NO ONE WILL TELL ME HOW TO START A REVOLUTION

Luke Barnes

NO ONE WILL TELL ME HOW TO
START A REVOLUTION

OBERON BOOKS
LONDON

WWW.OBERONBOOKS.COM

First published in 2017 by Oberon Books Ltd
521 Caledonian Road, London N7 9RH
Tel: +44 (0) 20 7607 3637 / Fax: +44 (0) 20 7607 3629
e-mail: info@oberonbooks.com
www.oberonbooks.com

A catalogue record for this book is available from the British
Library.

PB ISBN: 9781786822796
E ISBN: 9781786822802

Dedicated to the memory of Anne Webb;
Head of English at Range High School, Formby.
Teacher at the school from 1986 until 2009.

This play is for her and all the other teachers,
like my mum, that dedicated themselves to the students,
no matter who those students are.

This play would never have been written if it wasn't for the support of a number of organizations and individuals.

This Play was originally developed through the Leverhulme Writers on Attachment Scheme at the Liverpool Everyman and Playhouse and I'd like to thank Lindsay Rodden, Nick Bagnell and Gemma Bodinetz for their invaluable support during the incubation of this project.

Secondly I'd like to thank Holly Race Roughan whose input has been invaluable on the development process of this play.

Also I'd like to thank Erica Whyman, Pippa Hill and Collette McCarthy at the Royal Shakespeare Company and the staff of the National Theatre Studio for supporting the development of this play both financially and in kind.

And finally I'd like to thank Anna Ledwich for her support along with Will Mortimer and Edward Hall from Hampstead Theatre.

This play would not have been possible without the actors, designers, directors and dramaturgs who gave up their time to workshop it, read it, and give feedback on it. These are:

Rita Balogun, Akiya Henry, Lashana Lynch, Catherine Rose Morley, Samantha Arrends, Cora Kirk, Daisy Fairclough, Joan Iyola, Kezia Joseph, Shaun Mason, Yana Penrose, Anna Spearpoint, Eleanor Rhode, Carissa Hope-Lynch, Rosie Vize, Rehanna MacDonald, Rob Drummer, Steven Atkinson, Hayley Greggs, Suzanne Bell & Meera Osbourne.

The first production of this play was presented on the 21 September 2017 at Hampstead Theatre Downstairs, London with the following Cast and Creative Team:

SUZIE	Charlotte Beaumont
EDWINA	Sophie Melville
LUCY	Helen Monks

Direction	Anna Ledwich
Design	Rosanna Vize
Lighting Design	Matt Haskins
Sound Design	Max Pappenheim
Production Manager	Tammy Rose
Costume Supervisor	Jess Richardson Smith
Associate Sound Designer	Chris Prosho
Stage Manager	Ella Saunders
Assistant Stage Manager	Danni Haylett

DOWNSTAIRS
HAMPSTEAD THEATRE

Characters

SUZIE

EDWINA

LUCY

They are sisters.

They are in a satellite suburb of a post-industrial town.

"Some are born great, some achieve greatness
and some have greatness thrust upon em" Malvolio, Twelfth Night

…. What about everyone else?

NOTES:

This version is written in the writer's dialect. In the first production we asked the actors, who came from different parts of the United Kingdom, to take ownership of the language in their own dialect. We encourage you do the same.

This is also rooted in 2017. If this is performed at a time where the producer finds the play relevant but the references dated please feel free to amend.

OUR HALF TERM, AUTUMN TERM – THE BIT WHERE WE ARRIVE AT THE BIG HOUSE.

SUZIE: Okay. We're sisters.

LUCY: Can't you tell?

SUZIE: I'm the oldest.

LUCY: Youngest.

EDWINA: And I'm the fucking middle one.

SUZIE: This is the story about when we move into a new, suburban town, to try and finish our exams in a good school.

LUCY: And it's not boring like a lot of plays.

SUZIE: Lucy likes plays. Could you give an example of a boring play?

LUCY: No I don't want to offend our lovely audience. I do like plays though – I like all written down stories – books and poems too. I think they sound better in my accent than they do posh – it makes every line feel like poetry.

EDWINA: Plays are shit.

SUZIE: Okay. Let's start the story. We've moved house.

LUCY: The new house is absolutely gigantuous.

SUZIE: Huge

LUCY: Nearly as big as this Moby Dick.

SUZIE: Oi.

EDWINA: It's got like a big fucking bath that's just a bath and a shower that's just a shower. Not a bath that is also a shower. That's a big thing for us. We used to have one of those nozzles you put on the

1

	taps that made a bath into a shower. And this is a power shower.
LUCY:	Dad sold our family home so we could rent this little pied-à-terre.
EDWINA:	Stop using fucking stupid words. He did it so we could be at school and we can like do all our dreams and be happy and that.
SUZIE:	It was a big risk for him. A lot could go wrong.
LUCY:	Yeah if you're pessimistic. If you're optimistic you might say a lot could go right.
EDWINA:	Well yeah but when you're older and that you'll understand that things never go right like you hope they only go wrong. So yano.
SUZIE:	Well. Dad had to try.
LUCY:	Mum wanted this too.
EDWINA:	It was her idea.
SUZIE:	And it's not about being rich.
LUCY:	Well it would be nice to be rich.
EDWINA:	Yeah but it's really about us… Yano… Finding a life we like. Yeah. And if we were to be rich that would be great. But really… It's like, yano, about finding ourselves.
SUZIE:	Right let's get on with the story.
LUCY:	It's got big bay windows like in *Midsomer Murders*, gravel on the drive, massive bedrooms and it's made of old brick, you can see the cement overflowing like a proper old Victoria sponge cake…
SUZIE:	It's like *Downton Abbey*.

EDWINA: No it isn't that's like a bit of a unnecessarily big image isn't.

SUZIE: Yes it is like *Downton Abbey* only it's not a manor house it's just a house with like four bedrooms.

EDWINA: And it's Semi-Detached

SUZIE: Okay.

EDWINA: And it's on a main road.

SUZIE: Alright it's just a Victorian semi on a main road. Ok fine. But if you go down the road, like in one big long straight line you come to these woods that are full of pine trees, and sand dunes and squirrels and it's magic. We didn't have that where we came from.

EDWINA: Where we came from some people here might think was rough.

SUZIE: Yeah. Is. It is. Rough.

EDWINA: Alright is rough.

LUCY: But that doesn't mean we don't like it.

EDWINA: It, the world we come from. Tell them what it's like.

LUCY: It's hard to describe it without making it sound like what people would probably think a place like that is like that.

SUZIE: Okay. Okay picture in your head the type of place that doesn't have a lot of money but the people are really nice. That's it. That's where we grew up. Okay let's take a second to imagine that.

The AUDIENCE take a second to imagine the girls' home town.

3

SUZIE:	Okay. Now do the place where we've moved to. Let's imagine a quite well-to-do area. We're not talking mansions. We're just talking nice houses. Victorian type houses. With grass. Tennis Clubs. Golf… That sort of thing. Okay. Let's take a second to imagine that.

The AUDIENCE take a second to imagine the girls' new home.

EDWINA:	Well that's us.
LUCY:	We loved it at home.
EDWINA:	Yeah was mint.
SUZIE:	At home people wanted to talk about things that weren't themselves.
EDWINA:	Or their fucking new kitchens
SUZIE:	Or how much they hate their jobs.
LUCY:	All their nice things – their home comforts. Yano like how good spiralizers are.
SUZIE:	I mean obviously we had nice things where we came from too.
EDWINA:	But different types of nice things.
SUZIE:	Yeah not like "nice things" like cars and that but it was full of different nice things.
LUCY:	Yeah no one had like a BMW or a Mercedes or anything.
SUZIE:	The dealers did.
EDWINA:	Yeah but no one had fucking… a fancy kitchen. Or like… A bird bath. It's just for show isn't it. What's the fucking point?
LUCY:	It was nice in a sort like experiential sort of way. Like it was the people really. Theo next door in the garden. Talking to him was a nice thing. Just

	chatting with his feet in a paddling pool smoking those little rollies.
EDWINA:	Shame everyone fucking hates us there now.
SUZIE:	Yeah. Everyone hates us there now. They think we're snobs.
EDWINA:	They think that we think that we're fucking better than them but really we think we're not because actually we think we're shit and we can't believe that Dad thinks this was a good idea because we know how much of a risk it is for him but he thinks that Mum thinks that it's what she wants so we can see why he thinks it's a good idea. We liked where we were.
SUZIE:	I mean the school was shit.
LUCY:	And it was full of thick weirdos.
EDWINA:	Yeah but we were happy. Let's be fair we did like it. And Dad was relaxed. Not like here.
SUZIE:	Yeah because before he used to do all sorts of things like… Put cling film on the door way so when you walk into it your face goes splat. He doesn't do that anymore.
EDWINA:	Here Dad's being really edgy. Like really fucking edgy. Like you can see the tension in his shoulders properly like fucking… what's that fella in the church?
LUCY:	Quasimodo?
EDWINA:	Na the something of something.
LUCY:	The hunchback of Notre Dame?
EDWINA:	Yeah that's it. What did you say first time?
LUCY:	Quasimodo.

EDWINA: Ha. Anyway. Back to the story. I think Dad's
            worrying about money and stuff for the new house.

LUCY: Yeah and with Mum and everything.

SUZIE: We'll come back to Mum in a minute.

EDWINA: Dad's working all the time with the roofs and
            that and when he's not on the roofs he's in Tesco
            stacking shelves.

LUCY: He's like Boxer in *Animal Farm* he does
            everything and getting no thanks for it. He
            actually looks a bit like a horse – he's got like
            big broad shoulders and big teeth – like the love
            child of Ross Kemp and Cilla Black. He's got an
            amazing like shiny shaved head – I love guys with
            shaved heads – he's so like big and strong and
            proud working so hard must absolutely melt his
            head. Dad reckons he can get loads of work here.

SUZIE: Better area. Though I find the people fucking
            weird here, yano. When they get something nice
            something weird happens because they don't
            just… become happy with it. They start to want
            more little nice things and in the end they spend
            all their time getting more little nice things and
            they forget what they wanted in the first place.
            It just becomes like about getting more stuff that
            doesn't actually… Do anything.

EDWINA: Yeah but it's not like that with us it's literally just
            Dad working so we can stay here.

LUCY: All he does is work and look after Mum.

EDWINA: We're not talking about that yet. All I'm thinking
            about is when we get great jobs and go to uni
            because we went to a good school and we can
            pay his and Mum's rent so they can live here
            and be happy and that.

SUZIE: That's what we need to keep reminding
           ourselves of.

LUCY: Look how happy it makes Mum and Dad being
           here. Even though Dad's stopped doing loads
           of things like going to the pub three times a
           week they're happy. They probably lie in bed
           every night imagining me being picked up for
           prom on the drive. Some big tall handsome man
           driving up in a white limo, suit on, I can see him
           now, he smiles at me as I walk out in my blue
           dress (blue makes my eyes look mint) and I step
           in and we drive off. Drive away into the sunset.
           Like Heathcliff and Cathy in a disco hummer
           playing Kate Bush. And when we're old we'll
           come back from our rare monkey sanctuary and
           do secret millionaire to all our friends. That's
           what they go to bed thinking about.

SUZIE: But the point is now that we're at a good school
           there is a 'wealth of possibility.'

EDWINA: I want to be like… a fucking banker. high.
           low. high. low. money. bang. hookers. bang.
           boss. Walk in like fucking Jordan Belfour and
           have everyone go "yeahhhhhh" and I'm like
           "yeahhhh" and everyone's like "yeahhh" and
           everyone loves me. And everyone respects me
           because I'm fucking rich.

SUZIE: I just want to do the best I can.

EDWINA: Jesus Christ.

SUZIE: What?

EDWINA: That's the fucking lamest thing you could have
           said then.

SUZIE: Shut up! Mum's really thin but there's nothing
           we can do.

LUCY:	When she was a flowering rose she used to look like Suzie.
SUZIE:	She used to be so big and healthy.
LUCY:	Really into baking like Marry Berry.
EDWINA:	Coming home to the smell of apple pie and then by tea she would have eaten it. Pure like crumbs in her muzzy.
LUCY:	Yeah and then she'd blame Dad and he'd go along with it because he knew it would make her feel less guilty. So he'd be sitting there apologizing for eating the pie with Mum having apple dripping down her three chins.
SUZIE:	She made the best apple pie. It's a family recipe. I've lost it now. I remember her saying something about Gammon.
EDWINA:	She looks like… really thin but like cocaine thin not like Rachel from *Friends* thin. And she's probably going to die.
LUCY:	She's not. Don't say that she's not going to die.
SUZIE:	Mum's sick. She's been sick for years. I don't know what it's called she's got but she's just like deteriorating. Like wasting. I hope she gets better enough soon to go out or something but now she doesn't leave bed and Dad won't let us go in. I take some like dead good pictures on my phone and give it to Dad to show her at bed time.

She shows the audience some pictures on her phone of the squirrels and ducks.

| SUZIE: | If something happens to Mum then I'm… Yano. The woman. |
| EDWINA: | I can't stand thinking about Dad growing old alone if Mum dies. |

LUCY:	But she's not going to.
SUZIE:	Dad's trying to hide her from us. He's only letting us see her when she's well, when she can look okay.
LUCY:	After about a week Dad calls a meeting.
SUZIE:	Dad never even speaks yet alone calls a meeting so I'm getting ready to comfort them because I think he's about to tell us that Mum's dead.
EDWINA:	We're all shitting ourselves. Poo in our knickers.
SUZIE:	Dad stands in our new front room.
EDWINA:	By the book case
LUCY:	By the fire. Taking some pose like some Dickens character who's about to tell some povvo kid that he's entitled to a fortune. He might as well be holding a glass of whisky but he's not he's just wearing his pyjamas, his minion slippers, and has a glass of full fat milk instead.
EDWINA:	And he looks at us. And he says This isn't home. These people don't want you here. So it's your job to change their minds. Don't fuck it up. That's it. And he says good night just goes back up to Mum.
LUCY:	His minion slippers treading up the hall to find their place under the bed.
SUSIE:	We don't believe him.
EDWINA:	Na that's just fucking stupid.
LUCY:	No. No one actually thinks like that. Do they.

WHEN WE START SCHOOL.

LUCY: It's our first day,

EDWINA: We're nervous,

SUSIE: Sweaty hands

EDWINA: Lots of farts.

LUCY: One of those days that the air blows crisp across the town, all the trees are waving like bending sideways in the wind, bent double backed over like old people.

EDWINA: The new school is nice

LUCY: Not like Hogwarts nice – but like… nice, muggle school nice. Dad thinks it could be great for me because I'm in all the top sets. He thinks I could get into Oxford or something like Slyvia Plath and then maybe I can write poems or something.

EDWINA: I'm not in the top sets but I'm hoping to do something I like at university that will provide me with a stable income.

SUZIE: It's not private but it's posh.

LUCY: The teachers are nice.

SUZIE: Mr McMillan, the head, makes jokes like:

LUCY: *(As Mr McMillan.)* Won't you talk properly you're not in The Stone Roses.

EDWINA: And none of us have any idea who that is.

LUCY: Dad says "a bunch of arrogant no marks from Manchester with cheap haircuts".

EDWINA: But it didn't really illuminate who they are for us.

SUZIE:	When we first arrived he had a big smile and said:
LUCY:	*(As Mr McMillan.)* Welcome to Grange High School ladies. Smells a bit like piss but it's alright I promise.
SUZIE:	He's really funny.
EDWINA:	Yeah.
LUCY:	He listens. Makes you feel like you're a person not just a student. Like a proper grown up. Makes you wanna wear like... pencil skirts and actually wear sets of matching underwear.
SUZIE:	The teachers here are properly good.
EDWINA:	They're so good that if they were at our old school then people might do stuff with their lives. It's backwards. Everyone here will be fine because their parents are loaded and have loads of mates that can get their kids jobs. But at home... People could like really do with really good teachers. They're all fucked unless they win the lottery or like... Fucking Prince Harry falls in love with them or something.
SUZIE:	The school's nice but it's full of wankers.
LUCY:	There's a guy in my class called Kyle who's like a proper Heathcliff but the only problem he wears tank-tops.
EDWINA:	Anyone who wears a tank top is wanker or a virgin. There's no one here wearing a tank top is there? No? Good. Anyone who wears a wank top is a wanker or a virgin.
LUCY:	Kyle Beasley is Mrs. Beasley's son. She runs Mrs. Beasley's Organic Food Shop.

EDWINA: She doesn't like it when you stand outside for too long. She gets the girl who works behind the counter to ask you to move along. That's the type of cunt Mrs. Beasley is.

LUCY: There's a girl in my class called Sarah-Jane and she's not a wanker. She's like the... Emma Stone of high school.

EDWINA: Emma Stone?

LUCY: Yeah.

EDWINA: Fair enough – I think she's more like Amanda Holden.

SUZIE: She's a mean girl.

LUCY: Yeah but she's nice. I'm scared to talk to her.

EDWINA: I think people are scared to talk to me. At lunch I get some chicken with me dinner pass and a group of boys laugh. James Micheals and his band of bellends. Bals with their north face on and fake accents. Sorry a bal is like a fake scal, like the type that was born in a nice house but chooses to wear clothes entirely from Sports Direct. I don't know if they're laughing because I'm on school dinners and all I'm thinking is FUCK OFF YOU BALS, IT DOESN'T WORK WHEN YOU LIVE IN A BIG HOUSE AND YOUR DAD'S A DOCTOR. I have no friends. And in this school full of posh kids I feel out of place – I know they're thinking "look at that chav on dinners with her shit trainers" I can feel it. Burning in back of my head right here. I feel like a monkey that's got out of the zoo and is wondering around the customers and no one's noticed I'm a monkey so they're all still staring... or something.

SUZIE:	Wina.
EDWINA:	What?
SUSIE:	Don't say chavs.
EDWINA:	Sorry.
SUZIE:	Mum says chav's the poor people equivalent of the n word.
EDWARD:	Alright. I said I'm sorry. Get on with it.
SUZIE:	Literally no one speaks to me. It's really depressing. It's like being a new fish in a tank or something that's like a breed no one's seen before. Is there something wrong with me? Am I ugly? I feel like Lindsay Lohan at the start of *Mean Girls*.
LUCY:	The girls are nervous to talk to me because I'm pretty and clever and I answer all the questions in English.
EDWINA:	Or you don't dress like them and you're really annoying thinking you're right all the time when actually you're just a bellend.
LUCY:	…Or that.
SUZIE:	Everyone is like really polite, but no one actually wants to spend more than five minutes with me, like I've got cancer or something.
EDWINA:	The girls are all like princesses and I can't be fucked with that so I go in guns ablazing with the boys. ALRIGHT BOYS WHAT'S GOING ON? They looked shocked to see a girl act like that. Mr McMillan walks in and he's wearing a pink tie. I know I need to say something right – something that will make everyone love me and think I'm the funniest thing in

the world. So I do. I go "Nice tie mate. What's
your name again? Mr Gay? hahahahahaha!"
everyone laughs and I get sent out but it's okay
because everyone finds me dead funny and
Mr McMillan is sound so he's not being a dick
about it so it's worth it.

LUCY: Hey Sarah Jane. Have you ever read *Wuthering
             Heights*?

SUZIE: Obviously she hasn't read *Wuthering Heights*.

EDWINA: I'm sure lots of you have read *Wuthering Heights*.

LUCY: You would expect rich kids read books.

SUZIE: She looks at Lucy like she's just asked her
             if she's ever walked on the moon with Buzz
             Aldrin.

LUCY: *Wuthering Heights* didn't work. So I try for the
             shit version. Plan B. Plan shit. Plan wank.
             The plan that no one wants to do unless they
             absolutely have to make friends. I put my elbow
             on the table and I say this like a brazen harlot
             Hey Sarah-Jane? Kyle's fit isn't he do you think
             he's got a girlfriend? And like Jesus throwing
             his fucking tables over in the temple suddenly
             everyone's really fucking interested.

SUZIE: I wish I was clever like Lucy, then I could just
             disappear into books. What do you do if you're
             just okay looking, not clever, not talented fat
             girl in a school where everyone acts like they're
             starring in *Mean Girls*? I eat lunch on my own.
             Like Simone and Pumba in the watering hole.

LUCY: Me and Sarah Jane are walking home together
             with some other girls talking about how much it
             must hurt being done up the bum and how the
             fall out must be terrible.

14

SUZIE: *(As Sarah Jane.)* Yeah so enough of that. You
            gonna ask Kyle out?

LUCY: No.

SUZIE: *(As Sarah Jane.)* He likes people like you.

LUCY: … What the fuck does that mean?

SUZIE: *(As Sarah Jane.)* Nothing. Got to go. I'll chat you
            on Whatsapp okay here's my number. See ya
            byeeeee.

LUCY: Even though they're thick as shit it's nice to be
            popular. Makes you feel powerful. I've never felt
            that before.

EDWINA: I walk home with James and the boys. They're
            fucking funny. One of them brought his dad's
            razor and is just going round shaving year
            sevens' eyebrows off. They don't hate me
            because I'm poor like Dad says… If anything
            they like me for it. They're like everyone back
            home. The only difference is they smoke and
            get fucked because they're bored where as
            everyone else did it to escape. I don't really
            know what to say but I know that I want to be
            in the conversation. So I think fuck it. I'll just do
            something Mad. Everyone likes someone Mad. I
            stand on the wall and I sing ANACONDA and
            do a little like Minaj twerk like this *(She can't
            twerk.)* and they all laugh and that's nice. If that's
            what I've got to do to make friends then that's
            okay. Singing and dancing for the boys, that's
            what I gotta do. Sound.

LUCY: Mr McMillan drives past in his second hand
            BMW and sighs. He's got a sticker that says
            Number One Dad Number One Teacher.

EDWINA: He looks disappointed. Fuck it. People like me
            for the first time since I've lived here. And it's
            nice. Fuck you Mr Gay! Wahhahahahay.

LUCY: What would Dad think about you doing that
            though?

EDWINA: Oh shut up you little shit.

SUZIE: Hey. Right. That's it I'm going to make a friend
            with someone, anyone. Mum always said that
            it's hard to be kind so I'll find someone that
            needs someone to be kind to them. There's a girl
            called Alex Corrigan who's ginger and gimpy
            and sits on her own so I sit next to her and I ask
            her how it's going and she looks at me like I've
            shat myself. What?

EDWINA: *(As AC.)* Fuck off.

SUZIE: Why?

EDWINA: *(As AC.)* Because you're fat and you smell and
            everyone's saying it and I don't want to be seen
            with ya.

SUZIE: You're literally sitting on your own, you're
            ginger, you've got braces, you're wearing glasses
            and you're drawing. Are you actually telling me
            to fuck off?

EDWINA: *(As AC.)* Yeah.

SUZIE: Because I've got an accent and I don't wear
            fucking… Scarves.

EDWINA: *(As AC.)* No. Stop being so fucking paranoid.
            You're all fucking paranoid with a chip on
            ya shoulder. It's not because you're poor. It's
            because you're fat and smelly. Okay? Now fuck
            off, lose some weight, and have a wash. I have
            drawing to do.

16

SUZIE: For fuck's sake! Dad literally just sold his house so he could struggle to keep us here and I can't even make any friends. Fine. Just get work done. I don't need mates. I'm just going to work on making Mum and Dad proud. I'm worried about Mum.

LUCY: She'll be okay. Won't she?

EDWINA: Let's get on with the story.

WHEN WE FIND OUR FEET AT SCHOOL.

SUZIE: It's after school and I'm waiting for Dad to pick me up in 2003 Skoda – he said he'd pick me up because I stayed behind for homework club.

EDWINA: Yeah well that's what she told Dad anyway.

LUCY: It was because the boys were bullying her for being fat and smelly and on school dinners so she just waited around for half an hour.

SUZIE: Shut up.

LUCY: But it's true.

SUZIE: Yeah but I've got to say it. Then I've got ownership of it. If you say it just sounds sad. It's about yano… owning it. Carry on.

EDWINA: Dad will only come after the crowd's gone anyway.

LUCY: He thinks that everyone will laugh when they see that he drives a 2003 Skoda.

EDWINA: He's probably right as well – people are like proper dead shallow here – like if you don't have least have like a 4x4 even if it's not a Land Rover the lads are gonna rip you.

SUZIE: I'd love to see someone laugh at Dad he'd put them through the fucking wall.

EDWINA: And if he saw anyone laugh at Suzie it would be like hello bang good night fuck off send my love to Jeremy Beadle.

LUCY: He wouldn't want anyone here to see him like that though – he's worried enough as it is.

EDWINA: He says any fighting or anything confirms what they think about us is true.

SUZI: Anyway. I'm waiting for Dad to pick me up and I'm looking out onto the field and a horse comes up to me. In its mane there's all these flowers, little pink ones like knotted into its hair, and they've put a pink rug thing on its back. She's got all this power, all this power and grace and poise. I can see the muscles rip through her skin and in its mouth there's this, neash thing, like what you'd put on a horse on when you're riding it but no one's riding it it's just there. I'm standing there slouched over like… I dunno, like some fucking receptionist. I want to stand tall like a horse, stand strong, be something, command respect – proper respect, and I look into its eyes and I go to stroke it… and it runs away. I watch it run through the fields, galloping so fast, the pink thing never falling off. Strong enough to knock down anything in its path but never forgetting it's a lady.

EDWINA: Alright fucking… Horse Whisperer.

SUZIE: Come on. Just let me get on with it. I start to go to the gym. There's an offer on a shitty little gym above Oxfam for £15 a month. It's shit – like proper shit – but it's worth all my pocket money because I go from being chubby to being lean – from being a fast food, TV watching girl to an active, intelligent slender woman. My stomach starts to form muscle, I can see them rip through my skin. My arms become toned, my legs become strong and I can run, jump, skip whatever… I take ownership of myself. And I want to do something. Something that's not Netball or Lacrosse or fucking Rhythmic Gymnastics. I wanna do something real. I wanna do something that's proper something that isn't fucking… girly.

LUCY: Okay Kyle's fit.

SUZIE: I haven't finished yet. I take an unexpected turn for a girl like me. I join a swimming club. I learn to tumble, I learn to crawl, I learn to reach and make my body move through the water. I learn everything – I feel a part of something, I feel noble, I feel alive. It's a meritocracy (see I'm not thick even though Miss Baker said I was). The best person comes out on top. I'm doing something that's changing me in my body and in my mind and my heart in a world full of anorexic arseholes lost in diets and make-up it feels fucking amazing. Who can? This girl can. And none of those cunts take the piss out of me again. Because I am good at something they see me an equal. And that… Is fucking boss. You guys have your friends. I have this.

LUCY: Okay Kyle's fit.

SUZIE: Fine *(Sarcastic.)* Please, tell me about boys, that is what I really want to hear, I love hearing girls talk about boys it's possibly the most interesting thing girls can ever talk about in front of people, everyone likes it and it makes no one feel bored.

LUCY: Really?

EDWINA: No it's not fucking Love Island get it over with.

LUCY: Oh shut up you lesbian. Fine. Back to the story. When I first saw Kyle it was love at first sight. I was almost like I could hear the violins playing and time slowed down in slow motion and ever since then I've developed like spidey sense – only like… Kyle Senses. And one day I see him walking home from school and SJ goes "there he is, do something" like the perfect friend she is. So what I do is I walk in front of him, just walk in front of him and that's it because I know my legs look good from behind and then, then, when I turn the corner I stop and I bend down to fix my socks, not enough to show him knickers but enough so he can see the top of my legs and then when he walks past I smile.

SUZIE: That didn't happen.

EDWINA: That's from *Legally Blonde.*

LUCY: That happened – it's not *Legally Blonde* it's life. I turn around and he smiles. He has amazing teeth like a shark from *Finding Nemo* or something. SJ calls me a slut but I don't care. It's because I'm clever and didn't just offer him to finger me behind the post office like she did with Robbie O'Neill. Kyle adds me as a friend. I didn't think a boy like that would like someone like me. Like imagine, one day, if we were to go on a date… If we were gonna go Maccies, he'd have to pay for it and I'd like to. I just couldn't. And it would make me feel like I owe him something. Which

would be shit. Kyle's mum owns an organic
health food shop that used to be an old pakki
shop/

SUZIE: / Woah what Lucy.

LUCY: What?

SUZIE: Pakki shop?

LUCY: What?

SUZIE: You called the corner shop a pakkishop.

LUCY: Yeah.

SUZIE: You can't say pakki shop.

LUCY: Why?

SUZIE: Well it's not a pakki shop is it?

LUCY: Why not?

EDWINA: Because she's not a pakki she's white. Get on
            with it.

LUCY: Okay. All the mums love it. And I can see –
            I'm like in awe of her. She's like the Michelle
            Obama of the town if Barack was a cheating
            blabbing shagger. She's so cool and wears
            glasses and scarves and that. I'm in awe of how
            she bounced back after Kyle's dad eloped to
            Lanzerotti with a tennis coach called Sabrina
            who apparently got into tennis because she
            was having an affair with Tim Henman and he
            taught her to serve and then they fell in love but
            she just fell in love with tennis. But I'm obsessed
            with Kyle's mum for bouncing back. It's funny
            because you would think, not like YOU but
            yano people would think that if you had to guess

which one of us grew up without a dad you'd think it was us wouldn't ya.

EDWINA: No.

SUZIE: People assume a lot of things about things they don't know about.

LUCY: I'm talking. It's raining. Suzie's just started staying behind at school for swimming and Edwina's off doing something else.

SUZIE: Dunno what that could be…

LUCY: Why are you telling the end of the story now?

EDWINA: Come on let's hurry up all these little interruptions are getting boring.

LUCY: Okay. It's raining. And Sarah Jane's sitting by the window and something about the pitter patter of the rain makes me see that Sarah Jane's so perfect. I think that Kyle would see her and take her and run away if he was into blondes and I want that. I want to be like Sarah Jane. I want to love and to be loved. It's obvious what I have to do. I go to Boots and I pick up all the shit they wear – all the Touche Éclat – all the foundation – all the glitter – all the fucking everything and I can't afford it so I look over my shoulder to see if anyone's there and I'm sweating and I wait and wait and wait and wait…. And I peg it out on the street and I turn to see no one's following me. Actually amazing how shit the security in Boots is. I stand in front of the mirror – I have an unquantifiable amount of shit on my face – I look like Cheryl Cole if she worked in Moulin Rouge but this is what they wear – this is what Kyle must like. I take a photo so that I can change my profile picture. I sit and smile. And I know that now, now I'm a

22

bit more like the other girls every thing's going to be okay.

SUZIE: Do you know how weird that is?

LUCY: Kyle – do u wnt 2 go 2 d pics on Friday? And he spells it like that do u wnt 2 go 2 d pics on Friday?

SUZIE: What is he, nine?

LUCY: No he's dyslexic. So don't be so judgmental no wonder no one likes you.

EDWINA: He's only messaging you because he wants to bang you. You know that don't you.

LUCY: …Shut up. *(Back to messaging)* Yes Kyle I do very much that would be lovely thanks. :) ;) xxx Fuck. I get nervous. My hands are sweaty and my breath is like shallow and my… Yeah. I'm excited. I dunno what to do. I go the bathroom and I go for a wee. And I see it. Fuck. He won't like… all this. I shave my pubes. Using Edwina's razor.

SUSIE: Lucy! These guys don't want to hear about your pubes.

EDWINA: And why did you use my razor!

LUCY: Sorry.

EDWINA: Okay fine. Now we're being open. I use your tooth brush sometimes when mine goes floppy. Okay my turn. After school I'm out. I'm out with all the lads. I'm supposed to be doing homework but fuck it these boys are funny. They're fucking funny and that's more important isn't it? To like enjoy your mates. That's life. I mean if you're not laughing you're not living and if you're not living then what's the point of being alive that's what I always say.

LUCY: You have literally never said that.

EDWINA: I have. It's a meme.

LUCY: Of course it is.

SUZIE: Right. So tell us… All those posh lads who think it's "really cool" to have a mate that's like "an actual Jenny From The Block". They're your mates?

EDWINA: Shut up your best mate is a big pool of water. My story. It's raining so what we do is, we hang around in the Factory to get out of the wet – the factory is basically a big abandoned factory just out of town, where they used to make coal and everyone used to work there and then when they stopped making coal no one worked there and now they all work in Tesco.

LUCY: Hold on.

EDWINA: What?

LUCY: You think you make coal in a factory?

EDWINA: Yeah how else would you make coal?

LUCY: You dig it up from the ground.

EDWINA: Oh fuck off ya smart arse prick. If you spend all ya time reading books and not having fun you'd know boring shit like that. Anyway – No one uses this factory right and you can creep in and it's scary, there's all these empty rooms. All the machines have gone so it's just like… empty massive rooms. It's dead scary. I keep thinking like – what happened here? Why did it close? Was it an affair with a poor factory workers daughter that made the manager be exposed for a paedo and have to shut down his business? My mind is like electric eels going all over the place.

24

It's proper secret, and we don't do anything bad we just hang out when it's raining.

LUCY: That's a lie.

EDWINA: Oi. My time. Be a good little girl and go and sit in the fucking corner. We'd go there after school; all of us in this haunted den. It's still near enough winter so the sky's broken.

SUZIE: And it's dark earlyish, that smell is out when the air tastes pure and cold.

EDWINA: And we'd sit there and just chat and listen to the rain hammering on the side of the brick. Everyone else thinks we're doing all sorts but we're not. We're just sitting, chatting, few tins, cheeky spliffs. That's it. Nothing bad we're not upsetting anyone – we're just in here, on our own having fun. And that's it. I have actual mates. I actually enjoy their company – it's the most I've ever felt like I belong somewhere ever. I'm happy. I want to tell Mum but Dad won't let me so he tells her and he said she's happy.

SUZIE: Don't you think it's weird he won't let us see her?

EDWINA: Let's carry on.

LUCY: Kyle is nice. He's like Prince Charming but without being so entitled and having a big blonde quiff. I wouldn't mind being his wife if he asked me. I mean how often do you meet someone that you fancy and is also your best mate. We talk about everything, about books, and music and we dance and it's amazing. I don't want to be friends with Sarah-Jane and that anymore. I just want Kyle. He's saved me from being one of those girls – he's reminded me who I am. It's not one of those things that happens

25

just like that. It wasn't like we're on a dancefloor or some pier or something and we just fall in love. It's not like that. It happens over a while. It happens after we've become friends. And I know you don't know how this feels Suzie but it feels like you just hang around with someone loads and one day it becomes easy. Then you know that you're friends and then one day you realize that actually all you need in the world is that person. And all you wanna do is see them. And all you wanna do is be around them, lie on their chest, and just breath in a quiet room. That's what it is with Kyle. They're the best ones, when you're friends first. Makes it feel… real.

EDWINA: You said you fell in love with him after he fingered you on the bench.

SUZIE: You told me it was it was after he fingered you behind the CDT block and Mr McMillan saw and gave you detention.

LUCY: … both those things happened after…. We became friends, we went to the pictures, went ice skating. I stopped caring about impressing Sarah Jane, I stopped caring about like looking nice for myself, I stopped thinking about Mum so much and learning stuff that I thought was interesting and I started…. I started like doing everything for him. Everything in my life, he comes first. But that's love isn't it. The heart wants what the heart wants.

EDWINA: What she really means is he told her he loved her so he could get his dick wet on the regs.

LUCY: No. It was more than that. It's love.

SUZIE:	Yano for someone who reads so much you aren't half thick.
EDWINA:	This is where Lucy forgets who she is.
SUZIE:	And she takes on a mask.
EDWINA:	She stops being Lucy.
SUZIE:	And starts being Kyle's "chav" girlfriend.
LUCY:	Shut up, your shoulders are starting to look like The Incredible Hulk.
SUZIE:	Yeah well. At least I'm doing something that would make Mum and Dad proud.

SUZIE'S FIRST RACE.

EDWINA:	Dad's here to watch Suzie. He looks dead fucking proud. Like all the things he risked moving here are worth it. He's sitting next to Mr McMillan.
LUCY:	*(As Mr McMillan.)* Hi there, that's my niece there. This is Tony.
EDWINA:	*(As Tony.)* Hello. *(As Dad.)* Alright.
LUCY:	*(As Mr McMillan.)* Tone sells lamps and is married to my sister. She's working so we've come to cheer on Olive. I won't disturb you. Nice to see everyone out isn't it. Would you like a nut?
LUCY:	Dad is still suspicious.
EDWINA:	He shifts around on his feet.
LUCY:	But smiles. Look at him. He's beaming. He's not saying it but I know he's thinking how much

he wishes Mum was here. Dad's never looked at me like that even when I got two 4s and a 3 on my yr 6 SATS. Suzie said he was crying but he wasn't, she was just trying to make me feel better.

SUZIE: I'm sitting in changing rooms and the smell of chlorine is fucking everywhere. I'm wearing Mum's swimming costume and it's about four sizes too big so I've got to tie it up with hair bobbles but I'm still shitting myself that my boobs might fall out. Dad says that if I win I can get my own one. It's embarrassing and I know it sounds silly but looking around this is why I'm going to get battered – not because of the costume but because they all have better teachers, better pools, better everything, they've been here doing this every day and night after and before school in better pools with better teachers since they were ten and they've probably got nutritionists and stuff – course they're going to batter me.

EDWINA: It's nice seeing him like that.

LUCY: It must be so good for him to see us actually do something

EDWINA: After all he's done for us. Oh, there she is!

LUCY: All the other girls snigger at her costume.

EDWINA: We don't say anything.

LUCY: We don't want them to think just because of where we're from we're violent.

EDWINA: We don't want to give them the satisfaction.

SUZIE: Okay. It's time. All the other girls are there. Waiting. I step out.

LUCY: Suzie joins the other girls standing like horses.

28

SUZIE:	I wish Mum was here.
EDWINA:	She looks like one of those bulldogs and she has a condom pulled over her head.
LUCY:	She looks amazing.
EDWINA:	For a knob.
LUCY:	All the girls look amazing. They all look like Jennifer Lawrence. Shaved legs. Designer costumes. Someone's gonna walk in and think they're models and offer them a job in Abercrombie and Fitch or something.
EDWINA:	James Michaels said that Katie Greyson, that one with the big hands, got offered a job in Abercrombie and Finch but when she wanked off the manager her massive hands made his dick look small so he sacked her.
LUCY:	I wouldn't wanna work in a shop anyway.
EDWINA:	Suzie's lost so much weight.
LUCY:	Yeah but her shoulders are awful.

A bell goes.

LUCY:	Suzie jumps in.
EDWINA:	And she's good.
LUCY:	And she pulls ahead
EDWINA:	All the other sardines behind and Suzie the eel pulls ahead.
LUCY:	But the big sardine with big hands comes in right up her arse.
EDWINA:	Kick her.
LUCY:	Don't kick her
EDWINA:	Do it

SUZIE:	Fuck me she's close.
LUCY:	It's close
EDWINA:	It's really close
LUCY:	And it's…
EDWINA:	It's…
LUCY:	She's…
EDWINA:	And…
LUCY:	And..
EDWINA:	And…
SUZIE:	MY BOOB'S FALLEN OUT.
LUCY:	Shit!
EDWINA:	This is fantastic.
LUCY:	Dad looks away.
SUZIE:	Just keep going….
LUCY:	And it's over.
EDWINA:	And we have no idea who won. Everyone got distracted by the boobs so we have to wait for the announcement.
LUCY:	*(As Announcer.)* In 1 minute 56 seconds, the winner is…. …. …. …. Suzie Johnstone.
SUZIE:	Yeah!
EDWINA:	But then something bad happens.
SUZIE:	At least Dad said something bad happened.
EDWINA:	We didn't believe him.
LUCY:	Dad said he overheard Tony to say to Mr McMillan

EDWINA: *(As Tony.) (Joking)* Who'd've thought chavs could swim hey.

LUCY: He was gonna take us to Frankie and Benny's but instead we just go home. Sitting there in silence. Hands like fucking grabbing the wheel so hard I think he's gonna grip through them and the wheel's gonna break and Dad won't be able to steer it so we just drive in a really long straight line into a lake. That doesn't happen. Obviously. Even Dad's not that strong. Dad with his eyes fixed on the road.

SUZIE: You could see Dad wanted to do something.

EDWINA: But he couldn't.

LUCY: Scared of being what that wankstain thinks he is.

SUZIE: And no one says anything.

OUR WINTER TERM. THE TIME WHEN THINGS GOT A LITTLE BIT COMPLICATED. DAD MAKES US ALL FIND WORK.

EDWINA: We've been here for like… five months now.

SUZIE: Christmas happened. It was tight. We all had £5 limits but Mum came down and that was nice. Dad is really stressed. He works all the hours he can at Tesco and then does every job as a roofer he can. He's ALWAYS working. I can't help imagining how lonely Mum must be. It hurts.

EDWINA: But that's how it is innit. Just get on with it. Until something awful happens.

SUZIE: Dad falls off a roof and slips a disk in his back.

LUCY: It's not like he's a paraplegic or anything. He's
               not like the guy in *My Left Foot*. But he's hurt.
               He's hurt enough to have to not work.

SUZIE: He's fine he's just like not moaning about it but
               he tells us he's been the doctors.

LUCY: Obviously he's not going to moan though – he's
               a man and men don't moan.

EDWINA: One of the lads said it was so he could stop
               working and claim benefits.

LUCY: What did you say?

EDWINA: Nothing. Just laughed. It's hard to stand up for
               what you believe without killing the vibe innit.

SUZIE: He can't work. And even when he's better he
               won't be able to go on roofs or lift things at
               Tesco. That's it.

LUCY: Well he might be able to do checkouts.

SUZIE: But he wants to be physical. Checkout ages him
               ten years.

EDWINA: All this is more expensive than he thought it
               would be and Mum can't, yano, Mum's not able
               to help. So Dad feels a bit fucked. Which makes
               us feel a bit yano… Anxious.

LUCY: He can be with Mum more which is good. That
               makes me happy. But it means he's going to
               need us to do stuff.

EDWINA: He sat us down at the kitchen table had this chat
               with us, well Suzie was swimming, conveniently. He
               bought some nice jam and bread and made a pot of
               coffee from a *cafetiere*. After about five-ten minutes of
               like bull shit chatting, skirting round the subject like
               Jimmy Savile's family at Christmas. He starts saying
               how he's going to need us to get a job, how he hasn't

32

earned as much as he thought and if we're going to stay here we all need to help. I ask him Can't we just claim some benefits. And he says no because we're not being the people that claim benefits it's what they expect of us. I'm like… fucking hell Dad. Get this fucking chip off ya shoulder ya daft prick. They don't hate us. Obviously I don't say that because he's be fuming. But I think it.

LUCY: Why isn't Hulk getting a job? How come we still have to work and she can spend all that money on going the gym and swimming.

EDWINA: It's because Suzie's the oldest and the fucking favourite. She has to train because she has something she really wants and it'll be all worth it if she does well.

LUCY: He didn't say that

SUZIE: I've got a job at the pool. So I pay my share and get the gym for free. So leave me out of it. Get back to the story.

LUCY: What about homework? What about Kyle? How am I going to do those well if I have to work all the time. It doesn't work. I have to get a job. So that evening Edwina and I set out to find work in our best clothes.

SUZIE: So she goes to the newsagents

EDWINA: They're looking for people to work behind the counter so she walks in and asks to speak to the manager –

SUZIE: *(As Manager.)* Hiya. What can I get ya?

LUCY: "Hiya, was just wondering, I saw your advert in the window and was wondering if it was still going?"

SUZIE:	*(As Manager.)* "Oh. No that's an old sign actually, sorry."
LUCY:	I saw you put it up.
SUZIE:	*(As Manager.)* Oh. I must have put the er… the old one up again by mistake. Getting old.
LUCY:	Okay. Well have ya got any more jobs?
SUZIE:	*(As Manager.)* No sorry closing now byee…..
EDWINA:	The search is really fucking hard.
LUCY:	No one wants anyone.
EDWINA:	We look absolutely everywhere.
LUCY:	Up and down the high street
EDWINA:	Right from the Village Inn to Pete's For Sweets.
LUCY:	We give CVs out at pubs.
EDWINA:	Tesco's.
LUCY:	Cafes.
EDWINA:	Charity Shops.
LUCY:	Takeaway Places.
EDWINA:	Every single shitty shop in town.
LUCY:	All we want is like glass collecting or washing plates or fucking cleaning shit off toilets or something – anything! And no one will even talk to us. Of course now I know they want people like them to work with them. Makes them feel comfortable. Or course they do. You read about it all the time – people trust people like them. Men hire men. Women hire women. White people hire white people and here – posh cunts hire post cunts. What else could it possibly be. But obviously I didn't know that then.

EDWINA:	We don't get anything. I tell the boys it fucks me off and they all sympathize with me and give me spliffs and tins. I think I'm getting a bit too into weed – I don't feel anything. That's dangerous. Then the paranoia hits in and I'm shitting myself that because of me we're all going to have to go back. James says he feels really sorry for me and says he's going to do me a favour. I'm thinking like – what could this be. What favour is he going to do for me? Is he going to buy me a maccies or something? No. He gives me a bag of green and says if I take it to some other boy's house he'll give me 20 beans. Like why fuck would I do that? I've never even seen drugs before I meet these guys, why would I do that? Is it because you think of where I'm from I'm a drug dealer? Or have like fucking…. relevant experience in this field?
SUZIE:	*(As James.)* Why won't you do it? I thought you were mad?
EDWINA:	I am mad.
SUZIE:	*(As James.)* Then what's the problem?
EDWINA:	Dad needs it. Mum needs it. Fucking even Suzie needs it. My whole fucking body is like resonating saying fucking don't do it but then my mind is telling me I should so… So I do it. I whack it in my bag, I AM MAD! LADS. LADS. LADS. And I fuck off.
LUCY:	They're only asking you because it doesn't matter if you get caught.
EDWINA:	What do you mean?
SUZIE:	You get caught no one cares. Some lawyer's son does and the world ends.
EDWINA:	Fuck off. They're my mates they wouldn't do that to me. You sound like Dad.

LUCY: This is the start of Edwina losing her identity.

SUZIE: The first of a few mistakes that lead her to being
            a twat.

LUCY: Which leads to her becoming something else,
            not a twat, just something else.

EDWINA: It's just green, it's nothing. I get back, job done,
            he gets a text saying he received it and I get
            twenty beans. And that's fine isn't it. Just being a
            lad. No biggie.

LUCY: Like pyramid schemes it's a really sensible and
            efficient way to earn money.

EDWINA: I feel bad. I lie to Dad. I tell him I've got a job
            cash in hand at the factory.

LUCY: It's true in a way in a sort of objective way.

EDWINA: He doesn't even question it. He's too tired.
            His back's fucked. And Mum. Mum! It's like
            she's been ill for so long that I've taken her for
            granted – she doesn't even cross my mind but
            he – he looks after her every day. His mind's
            chokka. If he knew I was doing that he would
            kill me and then kill all of them.

SUZIE: Mum would too.

LUCY: Mum came from a really intense Catholic
            Background. Any trouble like this is bad news –
            like cast out the family bad news.

EDWINA: She got fucking mental when I locked her out
            and ate all the chocolate and she cried over that.

LUCY: If she saw this. It would kill her.

SUZIE: All I can think about is making her proud. Dad
            thinks if I live up to my potential then it'll all
            be worth it. That doesn't make me feel nice it
            makes me feel… burdened. Like buckaroo about

a million things on my back I just wanna kick off. All I want to do is make this work for them. Make them know that it was right for us to be here. Make them know that someone's making the most of this.

LUCY: I'm stuffed. I can't find a job and I'm getting a bit desperate. I keep having these thoughts about having to go back to our old place and Dad looking dead sad and Mum sighing in her armchair again. I text Kyle. I don't ask him, I tell him I'm coming over. So I go to Kyle's and I'm crying, like rivers of Babylon crying, and in my mind I imagine his mum opening the door with a big tray of homemade flapjacks and giving me a hug and making me a cup of tea and we sit and watch *Loose Women* till he gets in and then him picking me up in his big strong arms and holding on to me and telling me everything's going to be okay. When I get there his mum is in a deep meditation so I go into his room and he's there with his cock out with a bit of salmon wrapped around the end for a joke, pubes everywhere

SUZIE: Lucy!

LUCY: It's an important part of the story.

SUZIE: It's not.

LUCY: Fine – put it away Kyle I'm not in the mood. And he sees I'm upset and asks me what's the matter? And I tell him. I tell him I can't get a job anywhere. And he says why? And I say I dunno, everyone else has got a job in our year. Everyone else that wants one easy, pff, me. No chance. Nada. Fucking nothing. None. Twats. I have no job and we'll have to move back and Mum's going to die and then I'll never be able to see you again. And he goes

SUSIE: *(As Kyle.)* Why didn't you ask me?

LUCY: and I'm all like why the fuck would I ask you you haven't got a job – you're not a small business owner or a stressed out chain manager.

SUSIE: *(As Kyle.)* I know. But Mum's always looking for part-time staff.

EDWINA: Part time staff usually means middle class white girls that get moist at the sight of a kitten.

LUCY: Kyle if I didn't love you and your mum before I love you now. I don't care that you don't trim your pubes, you're fantastic! I tell him that I'd love to and the prospect of working with his genius of a mum makes me palpably sick. I love him. In his eyes I see babies and marriages and funerals and everything – well not funerals – that's morbid but yano big events. Landmarks. I don't want anyone else but him ever. And I lean in to kiss him and he says

SUZIE: *(As Kyle.)* Do you think you could do something for me in return?

LUCY: What?

SUZIE: *(As Kyle.)* Could we fuck and you dress up in a track suit and like big up your accent?

LUCY: Do you really want that?

SUZIE: *(As Kyle.)* Yeah.

LUCY: …I start the job the next day. I work arranging like seeds and stuff on the shelves for these amazing like mums and it's amazing. I love it. I love being so close to Kyle's mum it makes me so happy. I love working and getting paid and being around all these fucking unbelievable women. They pull up in their blacked out 4x4s with babies and stuff, all looking proper

glamorous, looking proper like nice, long thick
hair, legs up to their face and I'm standing their
in my apron thinking I want to be just like that
so I tell Jane (Jane works with me) that I'm
going to work dead hard and end up just like
them. Jane's got a Master's in sports science
so she knows loads about the seeds and stuff. I
didn't know you can have a degree and a shit
job. I'm nearly getting paid the same as her and
I'm still in school. I love it. And I'm helping at
home. And I'm around Kyle's mum so I can be
the perfect daughter-in-law. It's win win.

EDWINA: It's all fine for her until one day she gets put on the
            tills and this woman walks in. Looks at the Manuka
            honey or something equally fucking wanky. Picks
            it up. Walks to the counter. Sees Lucy.

LUCY: Hiya. Are you having a nice day?

EDWINA: Puts it down. Turns around. Fucks off. Never
            comes back.

LUCY: Kyle's mum saw. She was nice about but she says
            she has a very special job for me in the storage
            cupboard. And that's fine I don't mind at all. I
            mean she's embarrassed of me definitely. But it's
            fine I get it. It's my job to make sure everything's
            in order and do replenishes – it's a made up job
            really and it's really degrading – but it's fine.
            It only exists because of Kyle. But it's fine. I'm
            doing a job so it's fine… No fuck it I'm upset.
            This is because she can't get over who I am. I
            think how easy it might be just to pop something
            in my pocket. Just to pick up some fucking – I
            dunno like fucking like… beeswax lipstick, every
            colour and just pocket them all and fuck off.

EDWINA: That's what they expect of us.

39

LUCY: She doesn't know I'm clever she doesn't know
             anything she just knows I'm not from here and
             my name's Lucy and that's it. And it's fucking
             awkward. I hate her. I can feel my hatred for her
             like bubbling up inside me. And then I think
             it's unfair that my mum has gone from running
             around making us food and telling us stories
             whilst his mum is walking around healthy as
             fucking Kate Middleton.

SUZIE: She doesn't like you.

EDWINA: Fucking obviously she doesn't her like what the
             fuck are you Luther? She wants someone posh
             for her son; not just some well-read chav.

SUZIE: Don't say chav.

EDWINA: Fuck. Sorry.

LUCY: Well I liked her. But now it's like she's opened
             up, showed herself and she can be who she
             really is. When I go around to her house for
             dinner or something she always asks me if I've
             washed my hands. It hurts to think that she
             thinks I need to be reminded of that. It hurts to
             think that that's who she thinks I am.

EDWINA: Like we don't know how to wash our hands.

SUZIE: Our mum would never have said that. It makes
             me feel sad that Mum might not ever get to meet
             people we bring back.

LUCY: I know. After dinner sometimes I go upstairs
             and fuck her son really loudly – really loudly
             so she hears just to piss her off like "OH".
             It feels nice like I'm releasing something. Like I'm
             letting out all this shit about Mum and having to
             get a job and all this stuff I'm keeping inside me
             that I can't say anything about and it's all just
             coming out. He keeps asking me to fuck him like

a chav. I say no. And I fuck him how I want. I do it like like ARGHHHGFHSFGHAHS like it's ARGHSO-HIGNGHSGF. Fuck you Mrs Beasley ARGHGISH –

SUZIE: Stop it. That's three times you've said inappropriate stuff now. Stop showing off and get on with the story.

LUCY: Okay. She heard it all and now she fucking hates me and I don't really care. She went from being my idol to my enemy and that's fine I get on with that until…. She phoned Dad.

EDWINA: You could see his face went dead dark. Like his eye's glazed over with fucking fume.

LUCY: He didn't tell Mum.

EDWINA: It might upset her.

SUZIE: Mum was always excited about talking to us about sex.

LUCY: When she's better she can talk to us.

EDWINA: Yeah. Shall we get on with the story? Lucy.

LUCY: So I have to have this conversation with Dad where he tells me that we've only just moved here and that I need to behave so that they don't think we're pieces of shit and that he's working his arse off and that I need to do the job because we need to stay here and all I can say is – Yeah well if Suzie had a proper job, didn't spend all her time fucking swimming, and you hadn't been so fucking shit, getting hurt and spending all your fucking time taking Suzie to fucking swimming pools, I could have a fucking life. We're suffering so she can do what she wants just because it makes you forget how fucking shit everything is. That's the truth. You love her more than you love us, you want her to succeed because it makes you feel better about how shit your own life is because you couldn't do anything more with it than be a fucking roofer. And then Dad's about to do a big speech starting with "I gave up everything so you could be here, so you could have this. You're an embarrassment! Why can't you behave? Why can't you just behave? Why can't you just keep your fucking legs closed!" When I say fuck this. I don't need to be spoken to like this I'm not some fucking slag. Fuck you Dad. And I run out of the house, like a runaway bride, down the path, past all these shitty little plants in pots he's got and I run – all the way to Kyle's. When I get there his mum opens the door and I just run past her – see you later miss, and I get into his room and I climb in his bed and just lie there. I go – I'm staying here for a bit.

SUZIE: *(As Kyle.)* Okay, how are you going to say thank you?

LUCY: He's being so kind. He's being so nice letting me stay. I dress up in a tracksuit. I scrape my hair back. I put on blue eye shadow. And he loves it. The harsher I talk the harder he gets. The dirtier I am. The quicker he cums. I hate myself. *(Phone goes.)* "Please don't quit the job we need the money."

Fuck off.

OUR SPRING TERM. THE BIT WHERE THINGS GET WORSE.

EDWINA: I'm making more money than my whole family put together and I think it's fucking selfish from the others. I've even started working at school because I want to show Dad how grateful we are, and I want the future.

SUZIE: Mum's become a ghost in the house. We never go in her room. I'm scared to see her. We catch glimpses of her sometimes when she goes to the loo. She looks bloated and ill. And all I can think about is how she used to look – how big and beautiful and loud and I'm shitting myself that she might never be like that again – I'm praying that she'll get better and we can all sit down and eat her lovely roast dinner. Dad says she'll be better soon. Doctors come and go – she's going to be fine they say. It's temporary.

EDWINA: She's just skiving off getting a job isn't she.

LUCY: Of course she'll be fine.

SUZIE: I don't think it's temporary.

EDWINA: Yeah well. You're fucking pessimistic aren't you.

SUZIE: Things never work out how you hope.

EDWINA: We don't know that yet. Let's stop talking about it. I'm making beans for Dad. I feel like secret millionaire putting money under his pillow like the fucking tooth fairy. He doesn't know. I'd do stuff like put twenty quid in his wallet. Nothing too big. Not so he notices. And I'd go shopping. Like run down to Tesco pick up loads of toilet roll and put it in the cupboard. Or when I knew we were running out of stuff, or had nothing in for tea I'd get it and pretend it wasn't me. And

43

he just forgets – he just doesn't even think. And it makes me feel good about myself. I don't know if it's right. It's making the world better though isn't it. That's all that matters. No one can pull me on doing anything wrong if it's making the world better.

SUZIE: For now.

EDWINA: All the boys think I'm funny and mad, like the other day I got this plazzie bag, filled it with aerosol and inhaled it all and passed out it was mental. James is beautiful, he's got like really blue eyes. Like proper blue. He's just got like really fucking good eyes… His eyes' are great. And he's been looking at me. Just to be clear what I'm wearing is normally like, jeans and like a t-shirt and a hoody, so it's not like checking me out because I look like a slut it's like *genuine* checking out.

LUCY: None of us are sluts.

SUZIE: Probably because Mum was so strict about this.

LUCY: Is.

SUZIE: Is. Sorry.

EDWINA: Alright. Shh. Mum could not give a fuck about looking good for men, She used to say "Why do we always give a fuck about looking good for men when they're just wearing t-shirts, jeans and shit trainers?"

SUZIE: But you don't actually always wear just a t-shirt jeans and trainers do you Edwina?

EDWINA: Well no but only because I've noticed what he likes. I'm not saying I dress for him, I just notice he likes it when I wear a tight top. For my birthday – someone got me a thong… Na I'm just fucking with you I bought it for myself.

44

	When he pays more attention to me he gives me more jobs which means more money for Dad.
SUZIE:	Did you ever think that he's just making you feel nice so you'll do stuff for him?
EDWINA:	I'm fit.
LUCY:	You look like a trout.
SUZIE:	Shut up you little prick.
EDWINA:	Stop. What I wear drives him fucking mad and suddenly I'm getting loads of money. Like thirty quid a day just for running with weed and a bit of chop after school and it's amazing. I meet him somewhere – look into his swimming pool blue eyes, take the cash, drop the stuff and come back and it's amazing. It was great. I was happy. He was happy. Dad was getting to spend more time with Mum. He was even saying she's getting better. It was perfect.
LUCY:	I'm still going to work in the cupboard and giving Dad money – I know if I don't we'll all be back where we came from so I'm doing that. I'm also spending nearly every night at Kyle's. I want to spend more time at home, I wanna help everyone, but I feel like I have to prove a point – Dad can't talk to me like that and he has to learn to respect me. And Kyle has this massive TV and loads of nice food and sex so…
EDWINA:	I'm standing on crannie corner, it's this like really dark corner that's in between these allotments and some houses where no one seems to live. The road leads down to the factory and I'm waiting for James. I'm wearing my low riding jeans and my thong. Little top. Juicy trackie jacket that says "lips" on it – I can't work out why like but it makes me feel sexy.

And then James comes up "hiya" I go, really smoothly – like twirl me hair a bit because apparently that's what girls do when they fancy boys but it just makes me feel like a fucking child asking for a lollipop. He gives me the usual, bags of green, bit of chop– tells me to go to this address and guess what happens next. He gives me another twenty and says you can have this if you want it. And I'm like freezing… I'm like what the fuck does he want from me, is he going to like… I dunno whack out some bloody knife and ask me to hide it for him… so I'm shitting one, stand-ing there, wind in the face, the thong fucking annoying me, fuck knows what's going to happen next and do you know what he does? He goes – give me a wank. I dunno what to do, I just look at him and his blue eyes are looking back… and I want to do it of course I do. But I ask myself like under any other circumstance would I do it for money? I know this is wrong but… We need the money. So I do it. I take him behind the factory and I do it, I know I shouldn't but he's so beautiful and I want him and if I can't have him normally then I may as well like this, I might even do it so well he might fall in love with me, and then there's Dad, Dad needs this, Dad needs the money. There's nothing more important in the world than having money… and if it makes me feel good about myself it can't be a bad thing. Feeling good, making him like me and earning money. Win fucking win. So I do it. It's the best thing for everyone. Even if I hate myself.

SUZIE: In the middle of this hurricane of a shit show I get good news. I got the trials for the trials for County. If I win them I can try out for England. England. Fucking England junior swimming. If

I do well there it could be OLYMPICS. So I'm working dead hard. If I can do this.... This'll make all of this worth it. I hope Mum makes it to see me.

LUCY: I've decided I'm going to marry Kyle and that's how I can guarantee my future here – by marrying him, he doesn't know yet but it would be perfect because he's great and I could stay here for ever, inherit his house and the organic food shop and maybe even give them a job.

EDWINA: James is fit... It would be bad if it was someone I didn't like, like as a person... yano, fancy, not that I fancy him it's just...he's alright. I don't mind doing it – I'd do it for free so I don't see the problem in taking money from him. And when I do it sometimes he looks at me, right in the eye, and we hold it and it's... it's alright. His dick's pink and it's weird. This is the first time I've been with anyone at all even if it is just wanking him off for pocket money. I can feel like a tingling in my knickers. I don't tell him, if I tell him he'll stop paying me and start taking it for free – I like it. I like him. But this is the best of both worlds. Get paid, do something I want to do anyway and make him happy... Make Dad happy. That's fine right? Is that fine? It's something that Marilyn Monroe would do I reckon so it's fine. After a few weeks James started bringing his mates down to the factory, more of them, ones I hadn't met before and they all brought twenty quids. I was rolling in it, I was turning over £100 a day after school. How many girls can say that? How many girls can say they earn £100 a day in a part-time job. All I have to do is wank them off, it takes three minutes and some of them are fit. Some are horrible. One's really fat. His cock smells like cheese and he's not got loads of pubes but his balls are abnormally hairy. When I walk in they all look at me. In my low rider jeans and thong and I feel good, I feel sexy, I feel really fucking sexy, one boy called Baz is here today and he's disgusting his hair is going and he's only seventeen he must weigh about fifteen stone and he's looking at me and he's literally drooling, saliva literally on the floor "I'll give you a 100 quid to suck me off" he says. I don't want to. I really don't want to. Close my eyes. And just fucking go.

THE BIT WHERE THINGS GET REALLY BAD.

SUZIE: After training I'm sitting in the front room watching *Love Island* and eating a fuck ton of chicken. I'm enjoying myself. I'm just like scoffing and watching this shit and I'm into it. It's a good show and just when the big proper bit's about to kick off and there's going to be a re-coupling and they're going to split up all the couples with these new guys Dad comes in and I don't know how I know but I know. I just know. He turns around and leaves the room. I put the chicken down and I stand up. I follow him upstairs. Step by step behind him. Down the corridor until he gets there. He reaches his room. He opens the door and walks in. I've got to take a second outside. Just a moment to like gather myself. But I do. I psyche myself up because I know what's happening. I know what I'm going to see. And I go in… And it's exactly what I thought. She's lying there. She's so thin. Her face looks hollow, she looks at me with these little sunken eyes and she doesn't say anything. She looks like here, right

behind my head, and she takes my hand, she looks
so peaceful and I haven't seen her in ages and it's
weird seeing her like this and I can't cope with
it and I'm getting… I'm getting… I don't know
what to say. What do I say? I don't say anything. I
just hold her hand and look in her eyes just so she
knows I'm there. And she smiles. And as she smiles
all I can think of is the apple pies, and the hugs,
and the games, and sitting round at Halloween with
her singing and her whole life flashes before my
eyes and I can't tell you how much I'm going to
miss her. I can't tell you how much she is going to
leave a hole in my heart that can never be replaced.
And then she closes her eyes. And falls asleep. And
that's it. She just goes like a fucking bit of steam
just disappearing in the air. I mean we've been
expecting it for so long but now that it happens I
don't feel sad I just feel…. Numb. She looks so at
peace and Dad looks at me and says how she wishes
she could see me do something, wishes she could
see me swim, wishes she could see me go to the
Olympics or something and I know it's supposed to
be nice but all I feel is pressure. Dad, why couldn't
Lucy and Edwina be here? Why was it just me?
They're going to hate me. And he just walks away.
He calls them both again. Voicemail. Fuck.

LUCY: I've got twenty missed calls off Dad. I'm coming
back from Kyle's – I go past the little plant pots,
up the path, key in door, I open it and Dad's just
sitting on the stairs staring into space. Our eyes
meet. Neither of us expecting to see each other,
he looks little, he looks shrunken like a little
old man. And he can't say anything. "Are you
alright Dad?" and he just turns around and walks
upstairs. I follow him, as much as I've fallen out
with him he's still my dad… and he goes into
Mum's room, I follow him in and it's empty, the

bed is made, sheets changed. And Dad hugs me. Not saying anything. Just stand there hugging. I'm numb. I hug him back.

EDWINA: I get back from the factory. I'm in the living room and there's some leftover chicken, so I eat it. There's a card lying on the table – H.COYNE – Funeral Director. I just break down, here and now on the kitchen floor, no one doing anything. Everyone's in bed. No one to talk to. So I creep upstairs and go into Dad's room and I go in and Suzie and Lucy are in there with him, cuddled up, hugging, so I creep in with them and for the first time the four of us are together, brought together by Mum. It's been so long coming but now that it's here… I don't feel anything.

SUZIE: Dad tells us it's better this way.

EDWINA: We'd all been waiting for it

SUZIE: Even though we didn't say anything.

LUCY: We make promises there and then the three of us.

EDWINA: We promise to work hard so we can stay here,

LUCY: For Mum.

EDWINA: To make Mum proud. And Lucy cries

SUZIE: and Edwina hugs Dad

LUCY: And we just hold each other. Because that's all we can do.

SUZIE'S 2ND AND FINAL RACE.

SUZIE: Okay so this is the big race, it's the trial for
            county that if I win I'll get a trial for a trial to
            race in the nationals and I'm shitting myself. I
            just want to make Dad happy. I want to make
            everyone happy. Right, now fuck off I've got to
            focus.

LUCY: Kyle's really excited, he's got a t-shirt
            printed saying SUZIE DESTROYS YOU
            and everything and he's going to wear it this
            afternoon to impress Dad. I don't think Dad'll
            be impressed but he might be, you never know
            with dads it depends on their moods. He doesn't
            like Kyle. He questions why he's with me. And
            why when I'm with Kyle I play up my accent.
            We're both excited about this afternoon.

SUZIE: Dad was so excited about this afternoon. He
            won't say it but I think he's excited to be
            allowed to think about something other than
            Mum. And if this goes well it means this whole
            move wasn't just a massive cluster fuck. This is a
            big afternoon.

EDWINA: I'm coming this afternoon as well. I managed
            to get some meow from James for nothing – I
            do meow now, everyone does it and it's alright
            because it makes me feel a bit better about
            everything else because it feels like a party and
            if it's a party it's not *being*. Everyone's got to find
            a way to deal with the hard bits haven't they. I
            didn't even have to do anything he just gave it
            to me, so in the toilet I do four lines, get proper
            messed up, psyched up to watch Suzie beat some
            steroid monster and go through to nationals.
            She's my sister and we're all super proud. Super
            super fucking proud.

LUCY: Everyone I love is right here.

EDWINA: Everyone's buzzing.

SUZIE: Everyone's eyes are on me.

   HORN.

LUCY: Not the best start.

EDWINA: You can do it Suz!

LUCY: Swim Faster!

EDWINA: Come on!

LUCY: She's fallen behind four steroid white whale monsters.

EDWINA: Oh fuck I'm buzzing. Is Dad staring at me? I think everyone's staring at me. Am I talking too much? I'm feeling very anxious. I'm going to drink all the water in the pool.

SUZIE: I'm falling behind.

LUCY: Come on Suzie!

SUZIE: FUCKING HELL COME ON.

LUCY: You can do it.

SUZIE: I need this.

LUCY: Kyle turns to me and he looks at me and he says…"I'm leaving. I'm moving to Bristol."

EDWINA: What the fuck I can't breathe.

LUCY: alright, I'm coming with you.

SUZIE: ARGGGGGHHHHH!!!!

   She hyperventilates.

   SUZIE finishes the race.

   SUZIE loses. By a long way.

SUZIE: Fuck. Fuck. Fuck. Fuck. Fuck.

OUR FAMILY. THE BIT WHERE WE TALK ABOUT STUFF.

SUZIE: Edwina OD'd on plant fertilizer on the biggest day of my life. What an absolute helmet.

EDWINA: It's not my fucking fault. I was trying to have fun. I was getting hyped up to support you – trying to drown out all the sad shit from Mum. Fuck me. Sorry for getting into it.

LUCY: Okay. Just do the story.

EDWINA: They take me into a room.

LUCY: We shouldn't even fucking be here.

EDWINA: They ask me what I've taken.

SUZIE: I've just lost my big race and all I want to do is be with Dad watching *Hollyoaks* and I'm fucking sitting here drinking piss weak PG tips because Edwina is a knob.

EDWINA: I can't look at him.

LUCY: He looks so upset.

EDWINA: I can't look at any of them.

SUZIE: We're just standing watching.

EDWINA: Some shit doctor gives me a paper bag and tells me to calm down. Calm down. Who the fuck is he telling to calm down I'M FUCKING DYING!

SUZIE: You're not fucking dying you took drugs in a public swimming pool on a Wednesday afternoon.

EDWINA: Everyone's judging me and all I can think is how the fuck I'm going to explain this to Dad.

LUCY: She's pissing me off. I don't want to be here watching her breathe into a fucking bag like a knob. Today was meant to be about Suzie. I ask Kyle to

ring his mum to drive us home and she does. I leave
Dad and Suzie to look after the fucking tit – I've
got something more important that an idiot to deal
with. She turns up ten minutes later in her shitty red
polo and we sit in the back. No one speaks. She's
looking at me in the rear view mirror – waiting to
catch me out giving crack to her son or something.
She puts on Radio 4. I imagine smashing her head
in. Just taking the headrest from the back of her
seat and smashing it right across her head, letting
the blood spill out all over my hands and my
face, cutting myself, smashing the glass and letting
my own blood out of my arm or something and
showing her, look we bleed the same now will you
stop being such a cunt. But I don't, I sit there and
watch the lights flash by overhead, one by one, right
over the car. No one mentions Bristol now. Seems
inappropriate.

EDWINA: Dad wait until we reach the car park.

SUZIE: *(Dad.)* Tell me everything

EDWINA: And I do. I tell him everything. And it kills him.

LUCY: When I get home later Dad is sitting in silence
            and staring at the wall like Miss Havisham.
            I drape my arms around his neck and lie my
            head on his chest but he says nothing. Just sits
            and stares. I feel fucking guilty, I feel so fucking
            guilty for not being there for him. He stands
            up, and walks out. I follow him, like a dog thats
            owner doesn't care anymore.

EDWINA: I can feel my family's world fall around me.
            The earth splitting open beneath our feet and
            swallowing us up.

LUCY: I bring Dad cheese and biscuits. Red Leicester,
            he likes red Leicester on a Jacob's cream

crackers with cut up apple on the side and some oranges. I say everything's going to be fine. Everything always works out fine doesn't it? Everything works out fine in the end, and if it's not fine it's not the end.

SUZIE: At least Mum didn't see me lose.

EDWINA: Dad won't speak to me.

LUCY: I try to tell Dad one of my best jokes "Dad. What kind of a bee gives milk?" and he doesn't answer so I tell him – "boobies!" He does nothing… just stares at the floor.

EDWINA: I let James fuck me. I've gone this far. I'm not getting paid for fucking or anything like that now. I just do it. I don't even want to. Get it over with. Dad's done everything for us and I've fucked it.

SUZIE: I'm supposed to be the woman of the house now. I don't know what to do.

OUR SUMMER. THE BIT WHERE WE DON'T KNOW WHAT TO DO REALLY.

LUCY: Suzie's packed in training because she's shit.

SUZIE: Alright.

LUCY: I'm just saying.

SUZIE: It's not because I was shit.

EDWINA: Tell them why you stopped then

SUZIE: If I'd have got in to those trials then then maybe but they've all been doing it since before they had pubes and they've got parents who pay for loads of stuff and they're just better. No harm in admitting it is there. They were just better.

LUCY: I was only joking.

SUZIE: Yeah well. Now I have to work hard at plan B, plan wank, plan shit and sit in boring classes learning about fucking physics. This isn't me. I've let everyone down.

EDWINA: No you haven't. They would have beaten you no matter what you'd done. Doesn't fucking matter does it.

SUZIE: Well that makes me feel much better.

LUCY: Kyle's mum sits me down over shit tea and biscuits. She's not the person I thought she was. She's not Michelle Obama she's Michelle from Destiny's Child except I don't feel sorry for her cause she's a cunt. She tells me about them moving to Bristol (he's already told me you dumb fuck) and I say Okay…Can I come? It's summer so maybe I can come over and help him settle in? And she says "yeah, but you'll leave at some point won't you, you'll break his heart at some point, so you may as well not come and let him get over it" and I say "I know I'm not good enough for your son. I want to be good. I want to be better. If you have it in you I'd love to come to Bristol with you and make myself good. My family are bad and I know you think that as well, I mean look at them. I want to be like you. I want to be good. Love him and it's summer and I'll have to come back for September anyway for school "and then you'll never see me again" and she thinks for a second and she goes "ask Kyle". She stands up. She walks out of the door. She walks into the kitchen. She closes the door behind her.

"Kyle, can I come to Bristol?" He looks at me dead in the eye and goes

SUZIE: *(As Kyle.)* I'm sorry babe.

LUCY: Why are you sorry?

SUZIE: *(As Kyle.)* I love you and that you know that don't ya.

LUCY: Yeah of course I fucking know that tell me why you're sorry.

SUZIE: *(As Kyle.)* I just don't think this is forever. You know. You're not the type of girl you marry.

LUCY: What?

SUZIE: *(As Kyle.)* You're the type of girl you out with when ya young. Like you're dead fun. And it's nice to be like naughty. But it's not gonna be forever. So I think it's best that I just, let go, yano. Start again. I don't want you wasting your time.

LUCY: But I'm not wasting my time we're in love, we're going to be in love forever aren't we. We're gonna get married and live here forever. That's what love is. Love is forever. And we're gonna have a kid, get a house, you're gonna get a job and I'm gonna look after the kids, that's what love is, that's what life is Kyle. Kyle. Kyle. That's what we're supposed to do Kyle can't you see that. Can I come to Bristol with you? Please? And he kisses me on the head and says

SUZIE: *(As Kyle.)* Sorry babes, we need to make a clean start, for both of us, start again.

LUCY: I have no one now. No one. Not like no boyfriend literally fucking no one. And my mind is a fuzz and I don't know what the fuck to do. I call Sarah Jane. No response. I guess she'll never pick up now.

SUZIE: I get called in for a meeting with Mr McMillan about my university potential.

EDWINA: *(As Mr McMillan.)* You did okay in your AS levels solid B's not disgraceful. You can still get A's and go to university.

SUZIE: What the fuck do I want to go to university for ya dumb prick?

EDWINA: *(As Mr McMillan.)* Suzie. Calm down okay. You calm? There's no need for that language. I'm here to help you. Right. I have one question for you: Wouldn't you like to be more aspirational?

SUZIE: What does that even mean? Aspiration is bullshit it doesn't fix any of your problems. Get a degree, get slightly less shit job, get a slightly less shit house, get a slightly less shit husband and for what? An extra 10k in the bank a year? You can fuck off it's not going to change anything for my family is it, it's not going to make me happy and with that I leave. I can hear him sigh through the door. The patronizing prick.

EDWINA: We are all fucked.

THE END OF SUMMER TERM. TIME TO GO AWAY.

SUZIE: Mr McMillan calls Edwina and Dad in for a chat about her grades and her behaviour.

LUCY: He says he understands it's difficult with Mum and coming to a new school and he wants to know what's going on at home. He says he wants to "give her the best support he can moving forward".

EDWINA: Dad looks worried.

SUZIE: We tell him Mr McMillan's nice and he'll want to help.

LUCY: Dad makes us go with them.

EDWINA: Sitting in his Skoda we can all feel Dad's nervous.

LUCY: His hands gripping the wheel.

EDWINA: His mouth really tight. Tension round the eyes.

SUZIE: When we get there Mr McMillan invites us into his little office.

EDWINA: Which is like small but posh.

LUCY: Not like everything wood and leather posh.

EDWINA: But normal posh.

SUZIE: Like there's a lamp from John Lewis posh.

EDWINA: And there's pictures of his shitty family everywhere.

SUZIE: Flowers that aren't because someone died.

LUCY: And he's being nice.

EDWINA: He shakes Dad's hand.

SUZIE: He gives us biscuits and asks if we want tea.

LUCY: Dad's being nervous.

EDWINA: He asks why we're here.

LUCY: And then Mr McMillan gets serious.

SUZIE: *(As Mr McMillan.)* Mr Johnstone. I'm sorry to drag you in like this but there's something we have to talk about. There have been some

59

allegations about Edwina from other students at the school before I say what that is, is there anything you want to tell me?

EDWINA: ….

SUZIE: *(As Mr McMillan.)* Edwina?

EDWINA: I don't know what you're talking about Sir.

SUZIE: *(As Mr McMillan.)* I can get the other families in if it would make things easier for you. James Michael's Dad is on the board of governors, he's in a meeting right down the corridor. Is there anything you want to tell me Edwina? *(Beat.)* Edwina. This is your last chance.

EDWINA: So I look at him. His little beady eyes watching me. Like a fucking dog waiting to be fed. I know that if he speaks then this is the history; that I fucked it. Because I was always going to fuck it, because of where I'm from, because of what I am. When that's not what happened. I had no choice. I know what you're talking about, we all do, it's all true. But it's not because I'm a stupid slag, we needed it. They offered it, I took it.

SUZIE: *(As Mr McMillan.)* Mr Johnstone, I hope you understand I can no longer allow Edwina to continue her education here after hearing that.

LUCY: Dad just stares.

EDWINA: And in that moment I see all the people in my family, I see Granddad on the docks and I see Grandma at home and I see all the uncles and cousins and family and friends and they would have killed for this. They would have killed to be me. We're the first people to have this and I've fucked it.

SUZIE: *(As Mr McMillan.)* You understand, I can't let her
              carry on here. I can't make exceptions for you.
              We can't be seen to be giving special treatment
              to disadvantaged children. We're happy to keep
              the others but just not her.

LUCY: Well we're not if she can't.

EDWINA: You should stay.

SUZIE: We can't.

EDWINA: Look I can work. I can keep us here, can't
              I Dad? Please. Dad. Please. Say something.
              Please. Dad. Say something.

LUCY: He just stares at his shoes.

SUZIE: *(As Mr McMillan.)* Look as I said, Edwina cannot
              come back. If the other two don't want to return
              then that's fine with us. I'm sorry. But right now
              I have to get to class.

LUCY: Let her stay.

SUZIE: *(As Mr McMillan.)* It's not possible.

LUCY: Well we'll leave too.

SUZIE: *(As Mr McMillan.)* Well maybe that would be best
              for all of us to move on from this.

LUCY: Why are you such a cunt?

SUZIE: *(As Mr McMillan.)* I'm sorry? What did you just
              say? Mr Johnstone?

EDWINA: Dad just stares at the floor.

SUZIE: *(As Mr McMillan.)* Maybe this is the problem
              if you'd discipline your daughters maybe they
              wouldn't be like this.

LUCY: We're just trying our best. Dad was right. You
              don't want people like us here. You don't want

us here. You are a cunt. You're a horrible cunt. You think we're dirt but you're too caught up in the *Guardian* to admit it.

SUZIE: *(As Mr McMillan.)* What if I do?

LUCY: What?

SUZIE: *(As Mr McMillan.)* What if you're right. I want my school to be a nice place for nice children. I'm sure you've got your reasons for being poor. I'm sure you've got your little stories. But still. The fact remains that this town is full of people that have got on their bikes and got good jobs and there's no room for your children to mess up their children's education. Actually. What if I don't want my children being around rough kids who deal drugs and shag at the age of fourteen? What if I think that every penny of tax I pay is wasted on chavs like you? Now, if you'll excuse me, I have class.

THE FUTURE, OR THE END OF OUR STORY.

EDWINA: We're at home in the front room.

SUZIE: And we can feel Dad's shame.

LUCY: The shame of failing.

EDWINA: The shame of being born.

SUZIE: The shame of feeling this anger that he can't do anything with.

EDWINA: What do we do now? Dad. Dad. Dad. Dad. What do we do now Dad? What do we do? What can we do?

EDWINA: And we keep asking him.

LUCY:	And we keep asking him.
SUZIE:	And asking him.
LUCY:	And asking him.
SUZIE:	And asking him.
EDWINA:	And asking him.
SUZIE:	Until he cracks.
LUCY:	Dad.
SUZIE:	Dad.
EDWINA:	Dad.
LUCY:	Dad.
EDWINA:	Dad.
SUZIE:	Dad.
LUCY:	Dad.
EDWINA:	*(As Dad.)* Fuck off! You've fucked it! The reason I wanted this for you was because I didn't want you to end up like me. I wanted out for you because this life is killing me. It's not the being poor; I'm not bothered about having a big house or a car or a garden or a holiday in fucking Malta it's the uncertainty. Not knowing when we were working next week. Not knowing how much we were working next week. I could work tomorrow and then never work again if some cunt doesn't like me. That's the truth of it. If they want to sack me tomorrow they can and we're out on the streets. It's the same for everyone at home. Why do you think they spend all their time in the pub? To be numb. You don't know what it was like for me and your mum. Not knowing if we were going to be able to feed you. Your mum who did nothing but want better for

you. The stress killed us. Look. You can start to see it in the lines on my face. You can see it in my shoulders. You can see it in the layer of fat in my belly. You can hear it in the tension right here in my voice. From the day I was born to the day I die it's the same for me, the same for them and it'll be the same for you. These cunts like Mr McMillan with schools that only kids in rich areas can go, grammar schools and fucking private schools... Those cunts keep those places going to keep us out. They'll expel you but will they fuck expel those boys. They'll be worried about their fucking UCAS too much. They don't want us anywhere near their Waitrose or their flat whites or their designer kitchens, their big cars, their big houses, unless we're washing them. They want us in the stock rooms where no one can see us. They do everything they can so we stay poor. Where are the libraries? The fucking Sure Start centres? They will always have everything and we'll always have nothing. And they hate us for existing.

LUCY: It's okay.

SUZIE: It's okay Dad.

LUCY: And he goes upstairs.

EDWINA: And we hear him close the door behind him.

LUCY: He's right.

SUZIE: What do we do now?

END

www.ingramcontent.com/pod-product-compliance
Ingram Content Group UK Ltd.
Pitfield, Milton Keynes, MK11 3LW, UK
UKHW020707280225
455688UK00012B/308